IMAGES
of America

BUCKINGHAM
ARMY AIR FIELD

History Connects Us!

This 1940s linen postcard reads, "Greetings from Flexible Gunnery School Ft. Myers, Fla." It features vivid oranges, blues, and greens and shows warplanes flying over a palm-lined street that is very reminiscent of McGregor Boulevard in Fort Myers. The Flexible Gunnery School was based at Buckingham Army Air Field and taught thousands of men the much-needed skill of aerial gunnery. (Courtesy of Lee County Mosquito Control.)

ON THE COVER: Aerial gunnery students at Buckingham Army Air Field near Fort Myers, Florida, are seen atop gun turrets mounted on specially modified trucks. Riding along bumpy tracks, using these swiveling turrets, soldiers could practice firing from a moving vehicle at a moving target—skills they would later need in the skies over Europe and the Pacific. (Courtesy of Southwest Florida Museum of History.)

IMAGES
of America

BUCKINGHAM
ARMY AIR FIELD

Chris Wadsworth, Matt Johnson, and the
Southwest Florida Museum of History

ARCADIA
PUBLISHING

ISBN 978-0-7385-8676-2
Published by Arcadia Publishing
Charleston, South Carolina

Printed in the United States of America

Library of Congress Control Number: 2010928636

For all general information, please contact Arcadia Publishing:
Telephone 843-853-2070
Fax 843-853-0044
E-mail sales@arcadiapublishing.com
For customer service and orders:
Toll-Free 1-888-313-2665

Visit us on the Internet at www.arcadiapublishing.com

*Chris: To my grandparents, Al and Marion Powers of Streator,
Illinois, and Eva Weinreich of Dixon, Illinois. A childhood
spent exploring the old books, magazines, and photographs in
your attics and basements ignited a lifelong love of history and
a deep respect for the generations that came before us.*

*Matt: In memory of my grandfathers by birth and marriage,
Col. Joseph Wisdom, Herbert H. Johnson II, and Sgt. Edward
(Bud) Miller. They lent their talents when their country
called, then lead exemplary lives their families cherished.*

CONTENTS

ACKNOWLEDGMENTS

A hearty thank you goes to following individuals and groups, who contributed to the creation of this book in ways big and small:

Lindsay Harris Carter at Arcadia Publishing, who kept us on track despite a number of "bumps in the road;"

Shelly Redovan and Brian Cotterill of the Lee County Mosquito Control District, who provided a fascinating tour of the former Buckingham base property and opened their archives for this book;

Donald Claytor Jr., also of Lee County Mosquito Control, for sharing many of the war-era mementos he has discovered over the years;

Shane Anderson, who shared his father's photographs, memories, and valuable Buckingham information;

Pam Miner, Victor Zarick, Gerri Reaves, and Harriet Winn-Smith at the Southwest Florida Museum of History, who helped locate the wonderful Buckingham material in the museum's archives;

Nancy Parrish of Wings Across America for her dedication to commemorating the WASP program and for the photographs and information she shared;

Film historians Greg Kimble and David Strohmaier for their help with the history of the Waller Gunnery Trainer;

Beth Koelsch with the University of North Carolina, Greensboro, who facilitated access to the Reva Ingram Fortune Papers, part of the Betty H. Carter Women Veterans Historical Project;

David Stallman, author of several military history books, including *Women in the Wild Blue*, which is about the WASP program;

Michele McNeil of Lee County Division of Public Lands for the road map of the base;

Lindsay Harrington with the Florida State Archives for her help with photographs;

Mary Kaye Stevens, a fellow Arcadia Publishing author who provided moral support and some tips related to Buckingham Army Air Field;

Tracy Jones, Christopher Muñoz, Anne Cull of the Cape Coral Historical Museum, Alison Fortuna with the Bonita Springs Historical Society, Erik D. Carlson of Florida Gulf Coast University, and Susan Hart with the Naples Municipal Airport;

Howard Yamataki of the U.S. Department of Agriculture's National Resources Conservation Service;

And the U.S. Army and the U.S. Army Air Forces, the predecessor to today's U.S. Air Force. Dramatic and historic military photographs are the heart of this work.

Most importantly, a tremendous thank you to the World War II veterans—living and deceased—whose memories helped compile this book: Stanley Vaughan, Oscar Corbin Jr., Georgilee "Hank" Elmore, Tommy Doyle, Dawn Rochow Seymour, Fred Schlosstein, Elizabeth Keatts Muñoz, Thomas Wilcox, Paul Fleming Jr., Robert W. Anderson, Carl Creel, and many others. We honor your service.

Unless otherwise noted, all images appear courtesy of the Southwest Florida Museum of History.

INTRODUCTION

The name James Everett didn't go down in history, but a simple day on the job more than half a century ago helped set in motion events that would change the history of Fort Myers and surrounding communities in Southwest Florida.

According to a 1942 article in the *Fort Myers News-Press* newspaper, Everett was the workman, a "colored operator" as the reporter described him, who excavated the first shovelful of earth at what would become one of the largest World War II military bases in the United States.

The work that began in May of that year was focused on building a "rim canal" to help drain away sub-surface water as well as run-off from frequent rain showers. Once that was done, roads were laid out, makeshift buildings erected, and concrete runways poured; the Buckingham Army Air Field was off and running.

With America headed into war, the demand for training bases was immense, and the army began building them at a lightning pace all over the country. Ten miles or so east of Fort Myers, the main mission at Buckingham was its Flexible Gunnery School, which trained soldiers in the dangerous skill of aerial gunnery.

In the early years of World War II, most American fighter planes didn't have the range needed to keep up with the army's bombers. This would leave bombers and their crews unprotected on lengthy flights over enemy territory. That's where aerial gunners came in. Sitting in turrets above and below the plane and at windows on the sides of the bomber, it was their job to shoot down attacking aircraft and protect the bomber so it could complete its mission.

Besides gunnery students, Buckingham also became the primary training center for instructors at the nation's other flexible gunnery schools. Late in the war, B-29 bomber pilots also trained at the base.

Over its 39 months in operation, Buckingham Army Air Field was home to hundreds of buildings, miles of roadways and runways, and all the accoutrements of a small city, which included the following: a hospital, a dentist office, movie theaters, baseball fields, swimming pools, a bowling alley, and the list goes on and on. Some 16,000 military personnel and civilians worked on the base at its peak.

Never forgetting its main objective, Buckingham saw nearly 50,000 aerial gunnery students graduate and head off to fight overseas. Advances in training were pioneered at Buckingham, and indeed, the curriculum was constantly tweaked and updated. The base was even home to an early example of virtual reality, with students firing light beam "guns" at "enemy planes" on a screen.

Stories abound about life at Buckingham, including the constant heat, the close calls in the air, and evenings of music and dancing at clubs in Fort Myers.

The "ugliest" base in the nation, as one officer called it, closed shortly after World War II ended. It was beloved by many but no longer needed in peacetime. However, the story of Buckingham Army Air Field doesn't end there. Planes still land and take-off at a modern-day airport at the site, roads once traveled by military Jeeps are now residential streets, and to this day, spent bullets, dog tags, old coins, and other mementos of that long-ago era are still found in the area. Even more importantly, the base spurred the growth of Southwest Florida—hundreds upon hundreds of veterans from Buckingham returned here to settle down. Some came soon after the war; others retired here later in life. Many went on to become local leaders, and each brought something unique to the community.

The goal of this modest book is to record a simple history of this remarkable facility that today is but a fleeting memory for the region's older citizens and, unfortunately, unknown to younger generations.

Through the valuable archival collection of photographs, military papers, and other memorabilia at the Southwest Florida Museum of History in Fort Myers, this book has been painstakingly constructed. Many more individuals and organizations contributed much-appreciated materials and information that have made their way into this work.

When dealing with decades-old documents, many faces have been forgotten and many photographs have gone unlabeled. Nevertheless, every effort was made to be accurate and clear and to only include items from the base at Buckingham, except where otherwise noted.

Chapters have been constructed that focus on the features of the base, the military men and women who made it their temporary home, the aircraft that carried so many aloft, and the brilliant training techniques that were all once integral parts of Lee County life. The final chapter looks at the many ways the base is still with us today.

Despite all the interesting artifacts, the book truly centers on the sometimes thrilling, sometimes touching recollections of nearly a dozen of our nation's veterans who served at Buckingham during World War II. They are recollections that are captured now and can never be lost, and the hope is that this book becomes a valuable and enriching window to the past.

One

Up from Swampland
The Base

In this dramatic 1944 aerial photograph of Buckingham Army Air Field, it's easy to see the scope of the enormous base with its web of roads and buildings. They're all nestled in the embrace of a three-sided apron and maze of runways. This was Buckingham Army Air Field at its peak. Thousands lived and worked here. Thousands more made short stops here, learning the art and science of aerial gunnery to defend America's bombers in battle.

This aerial photograph, looking east, shows the heart of the base in the foreground and the apron and runways in the distance. Barracks and other base buildings line the many roads. At the large traffic circle, one can see at least two churches serving the personnel at the base. If the camera was facing west, the trap ranges, the skeet ranges, and the moving target range, which was where gunners learned to shoot at moving targets, would be visible. The beginnings of the Buckingham Army Air Field (BAAF) were modest indeed. In 1942, Capt. Richard Duggan opened an office in a storefront in the Collier Arcade on First Street in downtown Fort Myers. In this office were a borrowed desk, a couple of chairs, and a typewriter. From here, Duggan and the newly promoted Col. Delmar T. Spivey oversaw the construction of BAAF. (Courtesy of Lee County Mosquito Control.)

Soon thousands of workers were employed at the rural site, digging ditches to drain away water, building roads, and putting up tar paper buildings. This work briefly caused a housing shortage in Fort Myers, and local real estate agents were put to work finding homes for everyone who came to the area with the base's construction. Hotels that were normally closed for the summer stayed open. Families let soldiers stay in their homes. This second aerial photograph shows a closer view of the eastern end of the base, which was where the runways were located. One can see several large planes on the apron, as well as the base control tower on the right-hand side. Portions of the long main road of the base leading to the runways are still there today. Now named Homestead Road, it leads to the Lee County Mosquito Control District's headquarters. Mosquito Control still uses a portion of the old airbase for its planes and helicopters. However, many of the runways have been removed, replaced with neighborhoods, or covered by underbrush. (Courtesy of Lee County Mosquito Control.)

Col. Delmar T. Spivey was Buckingham's first commanding officer, serving from February 1942 to early 1943. Originally from North Carolina, Spivey entered the U.S. Military Academy in 1924. He soon transferred to the fledgling air force and advanced quickly. In April 1942, he was sent to Fort Myers to create the new "Flexible Gunnery School," as the base's main mission was known. The 38-year-old project manager oversaw construction of the school and base and was soon appointed its commanding officer. Spivey left Buckingham to assume new duties with the U.S. Army Air Forces' Southeast Training Center. In August 1943, he was shot down over Germany on a B-17 mission and became a prisoner of war. He retired from the air force as a major general and became superintendent of a military academy in Indiana. Spivey died in 1982 at age 77.

This undated photograph shows the first officers of Buckingham Army Air Field. From left to right are (first row) Maj. Ralph Hurst, intelligence officer; Col. Delmar Spivey, commanding officer; and Maj. Walter McCarta, quartermaster; (second row) Capt. Richard Duggan, projects officer; Capt. Sam P. Graham, engineer officer; Capt. Harry Alexander, adjutant; and Lt. John Lambert, assistant engineer officer.

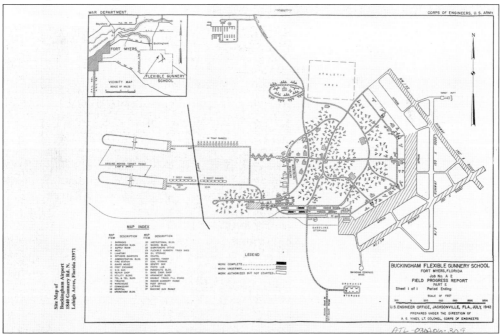

Buckingham Army Air Field was built at a cost of $10 million. It encompassed some 7,000 acres in rural Lee County. The base had a series of zigzagging canals that drained the water away from what had been swampland. During its peak, there were more than 16,000 men and women housed at the base and some 700 buildings—although some sources say there were only 483 buildings. The gunnery school graduated more than 48,000 aerial gunners. (Courtesy of Michele McNeill.)

Buildings such as these barracks went up on the base at a rapid pace. They were divided into the following two classes: those that needed to be finished in 75 days and those that were due for completion in 110 days. Southwest Florida is known for its afternoon rain showers, and indeed, poor weather conditions delayed some of the construction. Nevertheless, on July 5, 1942, the Buckingham AAF was formally activated.

This photograph shows some of the base's barracks. Tar paper walls, outdoor privies, and little drinking water were the norm early on. Stanley Vaughan of Cape Coral, Florida, trained at the base in 1944. "When I came to Buckingham, it was a totally dismal area," he recalled. "There were no flowers. No colors. It was all tar paper shacks. I was expecting Miami Beach, and it wasn't like that at all."

16

The photograph below shows the official standard for how a double bunk was supposed to look, certainly before the dreaded inspections. Despite the neat and tidy photograph, Stanley Vaughan remembers what it was really like. Originally, barrack windows were just holes cut in the tar paper. There were no screens and bugs were a constant problem. At night, damp air would come right in and settle on the soldiers. "You would wake up in the morning and your bedding was all wet," he said. Drinking water came from a lister bag, a leather bag hanging from a tripod with a spigot on the bottom. Due to Florida's warm climate, Vaughan says it was impossible to get a cold glass of water. (Right, courtesy of Shane Anderson.)

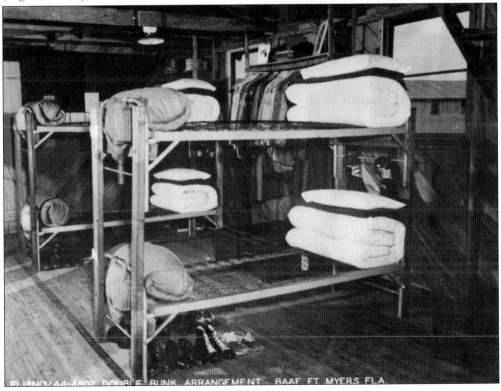

PI IRNOV 44-4802 DOUBLE BUNK ARRANGEMENT BAAF FT. MYERS FLA.

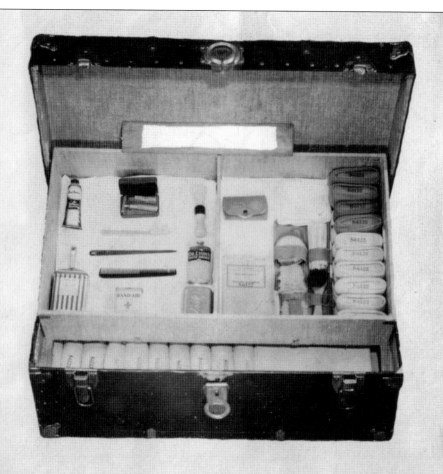

This unique photograph from Buckingham AAF shows the official footlocker arrangement for soldiers at the base. Just as their uniforms and bunks were expected to be neat and in order, so too were the soldiers' personal footlockers. Inside, one can see soaps, brushes, combs, bandages, and assorted creams and ointments. Veterans from BAAF say inspections of footlockers by commanding officers were common, and woe the soldier whose belongings weren't in order. The name footlocker came about because the boxes were usually found at the foot of a soldier's bunk or bed. Footlockers are often made of plywood, but during World War II, some footlockers were made of a type of pressed cardboard. This reduced material costs but also reduced durability in wet or humid climates. It's unlikely the cardboard footlockers would have done well in hot and sticky Southwest Florida.

Col. D. W. Jenkins took over as commanding officer of Buckingham Army Air Field in early 1943. Originally from Texas, Jenkins joined the army in 1928 as a flying cadet. He earned his wings the next year at Kelly Field in Texas. As he served and advanced during the 1930s, he gained a large amount of experience in the still-developing field of aerial gunnery. In the summer of 1941, while serving at Elgin Field in Florida, Jenkins was sent to Great Britain to study its gunnery schools. He brought back a wealth of knowledge and helped the U.S. Army expand into this field. He came to BAAF to head up the newly created Central Instructors' School—a training center for instructors at the nation's six aerial gunnery schools. Jenkins was promoted to commanding officer when Colonel Spivey relinquished command. Oddly, Jenkins was shot down while on a B-17 mission over Belgium the same day that Colonel Spivey was shot down. Jenkins was a POW until April 1945. He died in 1989.

(GI670-794F-BPS)(12-5-42-1P)(12)ORDERLY ROOM & SUPPLY BLDG. AAFFGS FT. MYERS FLA.

The top photograph shows an orderly room at Buckingham. An orderly room on a military base is used for basic administrative business, and there certainly was a lot to administrate at BAAF. According to a report by Capt. William Newton, a historical officer with the army, Buckingham Army Air Field technically covered some 65,700 acres. This included the Naples Airdome, a sub-base in Naples, Florida, where the P-39 airplane below was based. As with the main base at Buckingham, the field at Naples was constructed in 1942 to serve as a training area for fighter pilots, gunnery students, and bomber crews. Buckingham also consisted of two crash boat bases—one at Marco Island and the other on the Caloosahatchee River near the Gulf of Mexico. (Below, courtesy of Naples Municipal Airport.)

As the base grew, so too did a need to move supplies and personnel back and forth between Buckingham and the railway station in Fort Myers. During the war years, the railroad was one of the most common ways to get from one point to another in the United States. This was before air travel became affordable for most travelers and before the interstate highway system opened America up to motorists. To this end, Buckingham AAF had its own train tracks—7 miles long—running from the base to the Seaboard Railroad depot in Fort Myers. BAAF even had its own switch engine, a small engine used for moving railcars around. The switch engine was certainly powerful enough to push or pull cars filled with new students or supplies from the coast out to the base.

This photograph shows Fire Station No. 1 at Buckingham Army Air Field with two of the fire trucks parked in front. What appears to be perhaps a water tank or a watchtower stands on the roof. Between the many wooden buildings, frequent summer lightning, and the ever-present risk of a plane crash, fire stations were a critical part of base operations. Harold Horne was a retired Fort Myers firefighter when he spoke to the *News-Press* newspaper in 1991. Horne got his start as a firefighter at Buckingham AAF. "When I went to work for the base fire department, we covered a lot of crashes," he said.

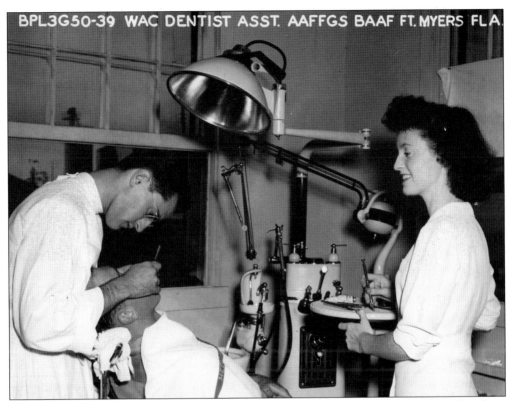

BPL3G50-39 WAC DENTIST ASST. AAFFGS BAAF FT. MYERS FLA.

With thousands of permanent personnel and thousands more men cycling through Buckingham during gunnery training, one can bet there was the occasional toothache, impacted molar, or broken tooth. There were also hundreds of wives and children of base personnel living at Buckingham. That's why BAAF had a full dental clinic with a large number of dentists and dental assistants. While it looks positively dated to modern eyes, the clinic was outfitted with the latest equipment at the time. The demand for dental services must have been great, as the second photograph indicates that there was an expansion of the clinic during the base's brief history.

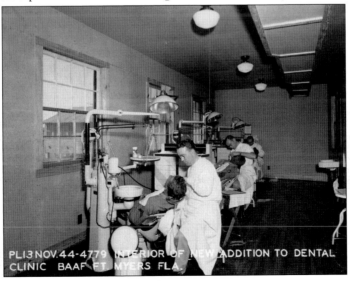

PL13 NOV. 44-4779 INTERIOR OF NEW ADDITION TO DENTAL CLINIC BAAF FT. MYERS FLA.

One of the first things new arrivals at BAAF needed to do was go for a medical inspection. There was certainly no room for modesty in the army. Stanley Vaughan of Cape Coral, Florida, remembers that when he arrived for his check-up, there was a big barrel of urine specimen bottles. Each solider was told to take one and fill it up right there on the spot. Vaughan also recalls being given shots at the base. At that time, the needles were screwed onto the syringes filled with medicine. As they were giving Vaughan a shot, the syringe ran out. They unscrewed the vile, leaving the needle hanging in Vaughan's arm. That was too much for the needle-phobic soldier next in line, and he passed out cold.

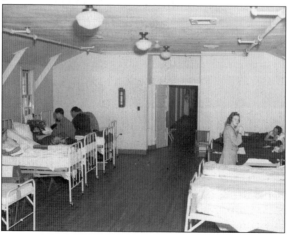

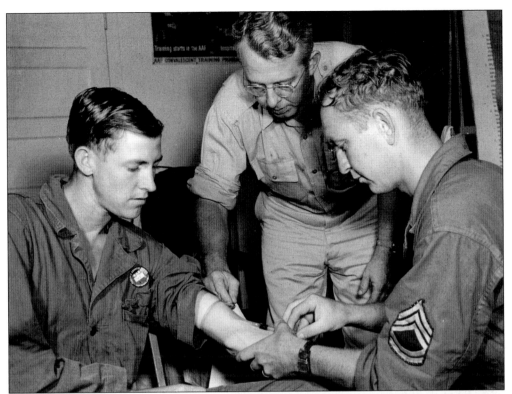

The Buckingham AAF hospital had almost 300 beds and was large enough to serve a small city, which BAAF certainly was. The base boasted a modern operation room outfitted with all the needed equipment. This photograph shows a base doctor, Captain Bartlett. At one point, the head of the base hospital was 32-year-old Col. Robert H. Looney.

Just as in a regular city, accidents occasionally happened that had little to do with military training but were rather just simple cases of bad luck. "I walked into the clinic, and there was a box with an arm in it with a wristwatch still on it," said BAAF nurse Georgilee Elmore. "It was an MP [military police] who had been in a car with his arm out the window, when another car came along and took his arm right off."

The drama could be heavy in a base hospital. Plane crashes and training accidents were not uncommon at Buckingham, and veterans recall that hospital staff had various ways of dealing with the stress. Despite ladies being present, this was the army after all, and army doctors were often just like other soldiers in some respects. "That's where I learned all the profanity, and some dirty jokes too, with the doctors in the operating room. That was fun," Georgilee Elmore said. "One of our doctors after he operated, he would sit in the corner and knit to calm his nerves."

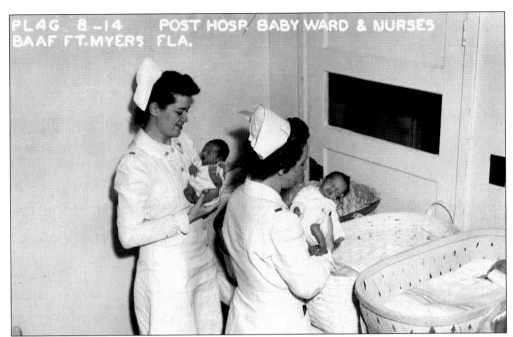

PL4G 8-14 POST HOSP BABY WARD & NURSES
BAAF FT. MYERS FLA.

Contrary to what one might think, the cry of babies was a common sound at the Buckingham Army Air Field base hospital. That's because many of the officers and enlisted men who came to work and live at the base brought their wives and families with them. The base hospital provided expert obstetrical care, and many babies began life at BAAF.

Indeed, officers' wives were a common site around the base. In this 1943 photograph, two wives attend a base baseball game as a jauntily dressed officer stands next to them. They are, from left to right, Colonel Graham, Virginia Spivey (wife of base commander Delmar Spivey), and Mary McWilliams. Their elegance and style—which included a mink stole—contrasts dramatically with the rough, sandy soil at their feet and the tar paper building behind them.

(G2546-794F-BPS)(2-12-43-4P)(63/0)
OFFICERS & WIVES AT BALL GAME
AAFFGS BAAF FT. MYERS FLA.

Here is commanding officer Colonel Spivey watching a military review. Other officers, as well as guests, join him on the stage. Spivey was rightfully proud of what he had built on this Florida swampland, but that didn't keep him from being bluntly honest when he once referred to Buckingham AAF as possibly "the ugliest field in the entire nation."

This photograph shows a state senator addressing a crowd at Buckingham. While he is not identified, visits by politicians to military bases are an age-old tradition. While Spivey may have thought BAAF was an ugly base, he appreciated the hard clay subsoil that withstood the tens of thousands of landings by heavy bombers. He went on to say BAAF was "the best army post that I know of."

Reviews were a common occurrence at Buckingham AAF and other military bases during World War II. A base band marched at reviews and likely also appeared at recruiting parades and rallies in nearby communities, such as Fort Myers. Reviews were a way to keep the men sharp and in top form, as well as a way to impress army brass, visiting politicians, and other dignitaries. "I guess [Spivey] just liked inspecting all the troops," said former BAAF nurse Georgilee Elmore, "If I could get out of [attending the review], I probably did it." Mina Edison was one such visiting dignitary. The widow of inventor Thomas Edison once visited BAAF from her Fort Myers home and reportedly even tried her hand at firing a gun.

PL7DEC.44-5118 BAND MASCOT "NICK"
BAAF FT. MYERS FLA.

This photograph shows Nick, the BAAF band's official mascot—apparently a terrier of some sort that enjoyed wearing sweaters despite the Florida heat. "We had everything out there," said Oscar Corbin Jr., a retired U.S. Army Air Forces captain who lives in Fort Myers. He was a gunnery instructor at Buckingham during the war. "There were churches, a hospital, a post exchange, and an officer's club. The base had about everything you wanted out there, except there wasn't the kind of girls you wanted out there. For that, you had to come into town."

Two

SERVING WITH HONOR
MILITARY MEN AND WOMEN

The men and women who worked and trained at Buckingham AAF were, of course, the heart of the base. While it was against the rules for this many G.I.s to ride in a single Jeep, it's clear this group from Michigan was having fun. Pvt. Stephen Jurinic is driving and Pvt. Eugene Kader is next to him. From left to right are Eugene Hubbell, Robert Guibord, Raymond Joseph, Aldon Mohney, George Bailey, Russell Vollett, Harold Heikkila, and William Amrhein.

Life wasn't easy for the soldiers who came through Buckingham Army Air Field. The Florida environment was extreme, the training was round-the-clock, and the future was unclear for the tens of thousands of men who knew this was likely their last stop before heading off to war. Nonetheless, in the spirit of the times, most did it willingly and proudly. "There were a lot of people here and they worked their tails off," said Brian Cotterill, who works for Lee County Mosquito Control and has studied the base's history. "In six weeks, they went from being a high school kid to flying over Japan or someplace. The blood, the tears—you would have to be crazy to not think about what it was like for these people in the wool uniforms just shipped down from Massachusetts or somewhere, with all the bugs and the snakes."

These photographs show soldiers wearing flight gear, which included oxygen masks. Since the aerial gunnery students were training to protect heavy bombers, they had to be prepared to fly at altitudes in excess of 20,000 feet. Despite the many frightening challenges ahead of them, soldiers met their duties with a fair amount of bravado. "We were young and damned the torpedoes full speed ahead. I didn't know I was going to live so long or I would have taken better care of myself when I was young," said veteran Oscar Corbin Jr., who was 92 when interviewed for this book.

This risqué sign with its double entendre slogan apparently stood outside the headquarters for Squadron N at Buckingham AAF. Images such as this, featuring pin-up style paintings of attractive women, were common during World War II. Similar images were often painted on the front of airplanes. This became known as "nose art." Some were naughty, featuring nearly naked women with monikers such as "Cherokee Strip" or "Male Call." Others featured cartoon characters such as Felix, Mickey Mouse, or Sad Sack. Within the rigid constraints and uniformity of the military, these images were a way for soldiers to express a bit of individuality for their unit. Military leaders usually just wink at such high jinks, although Britain's Royal Air Force banned such paintings in 2007.

Critical to the efforts at Buckingham Army Air Field were the African American soldiers that served there. Hundreds of African Americans worked and trained at BAAF, but an unfortunate sign of the times is that few of their deeds or responsibilities were recorded. In a large 1943 book about Buckingham, a page about the base's African American soldiers has the following headline: "These men do their part to train aerial gunners." On army bases in the South in the 1940s, segregation was still the norm, and photographs make it clear that BAAF's African American soldiers had their own mess hall, their own recreation area, and their own segregated units. These units included the 310th Aviation Squadron and the 956th Quartermaster Transportation Platoon. A quartermaster unit would have been responsible for distributing supplies and provisions to troops.

Carl Creel was a white officer in charge of African American soldiers at BAAF. In the documentary video *Over Here*, Creel said African American soldiers from the North had a hard time with the South's attitudes. "Some of the men were from the North and used to a different type of treatment," he recalled. "If there was a public water fountain, it was a public water fountain. But not so in the south. When World War II came along, we were still under the older customs." Creel had initially resisted taking command of African American troops. But eventually, he was quoted as saying they were a "fine outfit." He related stories of how his unit formed the first band at BAAF. When other base units formed subsequent bands, contests were held. His unit's band, made up of African American servicemen, won them all.

BPL3G50-32 CONTROL TOWER OPERATOR
AAFFGS BAAF FT. MYERS FLA.

This classic-looking photograph could have come right off a World War II–era recruiting poster. The enthusiasm and vibrancy sums up the "can do" attitude of the thousands of American women who served during World War II, many of them in the Women's Army Corps, or WACs. The corps was created in May 1942 and originally was called the Women's Army Auxiliary Corps, or WAACs. In 1943, the branch was converted to full status in the U.S. Army and became the WACs. Approximately, 150,000 served in the WACs during World War II. Other than nurses in medical units, they were the first women in the army. Gen. Dwight D. Eisenhower was once quoted as saying that the contributions of WACs to the war effort "in efficiency, skill, spirit, and determination are immeasurable." The WACs were disbanded in 1978, when women were integrated into other branches of the military.

Documents from the base say the first contingent of WACs arrived at BAAF on May 20, 1943. The first WACs came from Fort Oglethorpe, Georgia. At that time certainly, women were limited in the roles they could fill in the army. Most WACs at Buckingham originally worked as stenographers, typists, and file clerks. But as more men were needed for battle, WACs were assigned responsibilities in communications and radio operations, as well as driving staff cars and Jeeps.

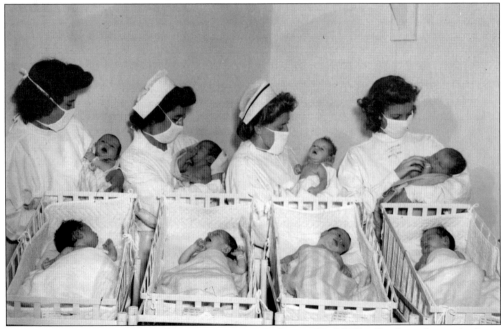

Georgilee "Hank" Elmore recalls serving as a WAC during World War II, when she worked as a nurse at the BAAF base hospital. She was there for approximately three years, nearly the entire time the base was operational. She went in as a sergeant and left as a second lieutenant. Her main duties were in the OB/GYN clinic, like the one pictured here.

Elmore remembers that the contingent of WACs was relatively small but was spread out across the base. "We had some in the general headquarters," she said. "We had cooks and chefs. Some of our base photographers were WACs. I'm sure we had some in transportation, driving cars, and some in the quartermasters. Of course, we had some over in headquarters as secretaries."

As every Floridian knows, hurricanes and tropical storms are always a threat during the summer and fall months. With scores of flimsy buildings, others made of wood, and millions of dollars worth of exposed airplanes and training equipment, the base at Buckingham would have been especially vulnerable to a major storm. During the period when Buckingham Army Air Field was open, base staff recall evacuating the entire facility on several occasions for approaching hurricanes. One of those storms was certainly the 1944 Cuba-Florida hurricane, seen in this image of a swamped street in Fort Myers. The category 3 hurricane killed some 300 people in Cuba and then accelerated over the warm Gulf of Mexico waters. It came ashore south of Sarasota, causing serious damage and ruining the citrus crop. Nine people died in Florida when the storm overturned their boat.

When a hurricane approached, once again the good people of Fort Myers stepped up to help, recalls Georgilee "Hank" Elmore, who was a WAC nurse at Buckingham AAF. "We evacuated the whole base, which included all the patients [in the hospital], the airplanes, and everything," she said. "We had two hurricanes while I was there. They evacuated everyone. That was something. It wasn't easy. Each unit was responsible for their own. We had ambulances that took people to the Morgan Hotel and the Royal Palm Hotel in Fort Myers. We took them over for our patients." The Morgan Hotel building still stands proudly on First Street in downtown Fort Myers. Unfortunately, the Royal Palm Hotel didn't survive long after the war. Once standing on the waterfront where a pink high-rise hotel building stands today, the Royal Palm burned down in 1945.

Another position that was sometimes filled by WACs was that of base photographer. Pvt. Miriam Lenig was one of those photographers. When she died in February 1993, her husband, Robert McVeigh, donated scrapbooks and photographs from her time at BAAF. Several of those photographs are seen here. According to notes with the donation, Lenig served at Buckingham in 1944 and was one of the chief photograph technicians for the base. In the years after the war, Lenig would become an art teacher and award-winning painter in the Tampa Bay area. She also illustrated several children's books written by her husband.

Just as many of the all-male squadrons and units had their own nicknames and logos, so did the photographers' unit at Buckingham AAF. This camera-toting, boxing kangaroo with a tough look in its eye was the photograph team's logo. Note the joey in the pouch holding a smaller camera or piece of equipment. Many of the dramatic photographs in this book were certainly captured by this photography unit, and many of those photographers were WACs. Their work as photographers is a good example of how women moved into roles that were traditionally dominated by men prior to the war years.

(G5109-794F-BPS)(9-25-43-1P)(63/8)
WAC OPERATING 16 M.M. CAMERA
AAFFGS BAAF FT. MYERS FLA.

There is little doubt that at least some of the WACs enjoyed celebrating and letting their hair down when work at the base was done. In local museum archives, there are a good number of photographs of WACs relaxing and even partying. "I had two friends and we did everything that 19 and 20 and 21 year old girls could do," recalled Georgilee Elmore, who was a nurse at BAAF during the war. "We would get weekend passes and go in town and play. We used to go down to the beach. We were pretty free after work hours. I got a weekend pass once and went down to Havana, Cuba, and saw the Barcardi rum place. We would go to Miami for long weekends."

Considering the discipline of military life, it's little wonder that many soldiers and WACs would want to let loose sometimes. They needed a release from their duties at times. Veteran Georgilee Elmore has very positive memories of both her time at Buckingham AAF and her time visiting Fort Myers. "We played as well as worked hard," Elmore said. "When we would go downtown in Fort Myers, we were really treated royally. The civilian people in Fort Myers were very nice to the military. Sure, we had a lot of wolf whistles. The men in the military were a bit more respectful. They were very, very sweet and nice to us. They were gentlemen as a rule." (Below, courtesy of Shane Anderson.)

Not all military women in the U.S. Army were WACs. There was a little-heralded unit known as WASP that has only recently started to get the recognition it deserves. WASP stood for Women Airforce Service Pilots, and it allowed women to pilot military planes. They didn't fly in war zones but rather filled critical stateside roles, freeing up male pilots for combat. These photographs show WASPs serving during World War II. The first is a group of WASPs at a base in Ohio. The second shows WASPs at Camp Davis in North Carolina. These images capture the spirit these women brought to the job. Despite their valuable service, it wasn't until the late 1970s that the WASPs were officially recognized as members of the armed forces. In 2009, Pres. Barack Obama awarded the Congressional Gold Medal to the WASPs. (Above, courtesy of Wings Across America; below, courtesy of David Stallman.)

PLI5MARCH44-2II VISIT OF J. COCHRAN CHIEF OF WASPS
BAAF FT. MYERS FLA.

This photograph shows famed aviator Jacqueline Cochran, director of the WASP program, on a visit to Buckingham. Cochran fell in love with flying in the 1930s and, after three weeks of lessons, had learned to fly. She went on to compete in international flying competitions and became famous across America. When she heard the army was forming a unit of women pilots, she quickly volunteered and became the head WASP. Women pilots at BAAF flew many of the tow planes that pulled targets through the sky. One of these WASPs was Elizabeth Keatts Muñoz. In an interview with the *Lewiston Tribune* newspaper, she recalled pulling the tow target with a B-26 Marauder while gunnery students aboard B-24 Liberators practiced shooting at it. "We'd tow the target up and down the coast of Florida," she said. "You got as far as you dared to Havana. I didn't ever think that it was so scary. I never had heard of someone hitting the plane." However, she did recall a time that the towline was severed by B-24 gunners, and her target fell into the waters of the Gulf.

Dawn Rochow Seymour was a 26-year-old WASP at Buckingham. Recruited by Jackie Cochran, she recalls the amazement she encountered upon arriving at BAAF. "The men at Buckingham were absolutely astonished that we were there," she said. "They stared at us. Who could these women be who were able to fly B-17s?" Besides towing targets, Seymour and other WASPs often flew with gunnery instructors and their students on long, five-hour training runs. She recalls one time a .50 caliber gun "jumped its pin" and hit the gunner right in the face. She gave the gunner first aid and made an emergency landing to get the poor soldier to a waiting ambulance. "We worked every day, either morning or afternoon shift, and had every other Sunday off, so we were needed," she said. (Both, courtesy of Wings Across America.)

While at Buckingham, Dawn Rochow Seymour was elected squadron leader of the WASPs. At first, the WASPs were only allowed to fly as copilots with men officially in charge. "The boys that we flew with, they just loved having us on board," Seymour said. "We would take off and do the landings for them." Eventually, the WASPs were allowed to be the primary pilots on flights. Seymour says Buckingham had great runways, despite the occasional alligator sunning on them. Flying in the area was an experience. "The sky was marvelous down there," Seymour recalled. "Every afternoon during the summer, there would be those towering nimbocumulus clouds. You would never fly through these storm clouds. They were like columns in the sky and you would weave your way to the gulf and back." The WASPs' time at BAAF came to an end around December 1944, when the army disbanded the service. Seymour, who married while at BAAF, went on to raise a family and work in the family business. She has stayed active in WASP organizations for decades now. (Courtesy of Wings Across America.)

This image shows a patch with the WASP logo, a female gremlin named Fifinella. The character came from the 1943 book *The Gremlins* by author Roald Dahl and was designed by Walt Disney. In her book *Clipped Wings*, Molly Merryman quotes a 1945 army publication that stated that while many women pilots were given a chilly reception by the men at some AAF bases, the women pilots in Southwest Florida were much appreciated by their male coworkers. "Buckingham Field was sorry to lose their WASPs. The men on the line and the air crew members who helped keep the gunnery missions operating had grown to respect the blue WASP uniform and also had grown to admire the women who wore those colors. A more enviable record could not have been left." (Courtesy of Wings Across America.)

Three

LEARNING TO SHOOT
THE TRAINING

Buckingham Army Air Field was the home of what was known as the Flexible Gunnery School. While there were always many things happening at the enormous base, its primary mission was training aerial gunners who would take up positions in B-17s, B-24s, B-26s, and other bombers and target enemy aircraft in the sky. New arrivals at BAAF underwent a rigorous and exhausting five- or six-week training session. Training at BAAF officially began on September 5, 1942.

While many might think the focus at BAAF would be on the skies overhead, in reality, much of the training at Buckingham took place on the ground. Skeet shooting on firing ranges with 12-gauge shotguns was part of the training. So was using .22 caliber rifles and .50 caliber machine guns to teach the men proper sighting. A moving belt with miniature airplanes attached to it was employed at one target range.

Soon, the gunners advanced to shooting clay pigeons from the back of a moving truck. The motion of the truck began to help the gunner understand the complexities of aiming and firing from a swooping and diving airplane. This photograph shows Robert W. Anderson firing a truck-mounted gun while his instructor stands next to him. Anderson went on to serve in Korea, became a newspaper photographer, and later opened a successful bridal and dress shop in New Jersey with his wife, Vera. He passed away in 2002. (Courtesy of Shane Anderson.)

Eventually, the gunners-in-training moved on to real gun turrets like those they would be using on various medium and heavy bombers. On the Jeep range, the gunners tested their aim with .30 and .50 caliber machine guns attached to spinning turrets atop trucks that were specially constructed for this training. The men aimed at large cloth targets that perched high above Jeeps on the range. The unmanned Jeeps drove in circles, protected by an earthen berm, while gunnery students fired away at the white cloth targets. The tips of the bullets were dipped in paint so that direct hits could be easily counted on the target. Scores were tabulated for each gunner. "We used to save the cloth targets and make towels out of them," said Oscar Corbin Jr., who was a gun turret instructor at BAAF and was later mayor of Fort Myers.

This dramatic photograph shows soldiers firing their weapons at targets on what was known as the silhouette range. Images of enemy aircraft were silhouetted on targets. Sometimes instructors would rig the guns to malfunction, such as beginning to fire non-stop. Many a rattled gunner had to diagnose the problem and fix it with teacher and classmates watching.

Veteran Stanley Vaughan remembers trying to learn to shoot from the back of a truck. "You had a ring around you and you were standing in the truck, and it went through the woods, so you were swaying from side to side," he remembered. "The clay pigeons would come out first from the right, then from the left, then low, then high, then two or three at the same time from different directions."

In the sixth week of training, pilots take off from BAAF with gunners at the ready. They fly over Fort Myers and out over the blue waters of the Gulf of Mexico. There, the student gunners practice air-to-air firing. Two planes pull large cloth banners behind them, and just as on the ground, gunners target these banners with paint-tipped bullets. Back on terra firma, the number of direct hits are counted and carefully scored for each gunnery student. "I flew in B-17s," said Vaughan. "I got back in the tail, and all the firing was done from the side position. There was a plane towing a target—a big, long, white sheet. The .50 caliber bullets were tipped with colors, and the colors went in and showed whether you were hitting the target or not. Some days were pretty grim."

BASIC GUNNERY TRAINING

LAST NAME / FIRST		MIDDLE INITIAL	GRADE	ASN
Mathews, Donell				14 203 472

ORGANIZATION	STATION	COMMAND
B-29 2117th AAF BASE UNIT Tail	RAAF, FT. MYERS, FLA.	AAFFTC

SPECIALIZED TURRET	SCHOOL	GRADUATION DATE
GENERAL ELECTRIC	FLEXIBLE GUNNERY	AUG 11 1945

TRAINING

SUBJECT	HOURS	GRADE	SUBJECT	HOURS	GRADE
WEAPONS, CAL. 50	19	4	GROUND FLIGHT INSTRUCTION	39	*
WEAPONS MAINTENANCE & MALF.	6	4	FILM ASSESSING AND SCORING	16	*
TURRETS	28	*	MILITARY TRAINING	24	*
TURRET MANIPULATION	32	*	OXYGEN INDOCTRINATION	11	*
SIGHTING	10	*	MEDICAL AID	10	*
E-14 TRAINER	70	—	ARMY ORIENTATION	12	*
WALLER TRAINER	12	3	PHYSICAL TRAINING	72	*
AIRCRAFT RECOGNITION	22	4	QUALIFICATION CAL. 45	2	*
INTERPHONE PROCEDURE	10	4	FAMILIARIZATION CAL. Carbine	1	*

TRAINING

SUBJECT	NO. ROUNDS	HOURS	GRADE	SUBJECT	NO. ROUNDS	HOURS	GRADE
BASIC DEFLECTION	50	2	5	POORMAN RANGE	0	0	0
MOVING BASE	150	6	2	ORIENTATION FLIGHT	0	2	0
TURRET SHOTGUN	0	36	4	BURST CONTROL FLIGHT	120	5	4
BURST CONTROL	300	4	4	AIR-TO-GROUND FLIGHT	120	24	4
MOVING TARGET, HANDHELD	0	0	0	GUN CAMERA FLIGHT	0	20	* 4
MOVING TARGET, TURRET	1500	20	5	FRANGIBLE BULLET FLIGHT	0	0	0

PHASE CHECK SCORES

TYPE	GRADE	TYPE	GRADE
.50 CAL. STRIPPING AND ASSEMBLING		.50 CAL. HARMONIZATION	
.50 CAL. PREVENTIVE MAINTENANCE		SIGHTING	
.50 CAL. CARE AND CLEANING		TURRET OPERATION	

GRADE: 1-UNSATISFACTORY, 2-POOR, 3-AVERAGE, 4-GOOD, 5-EXCELLENT

REMARKS   Nine (9) Phase Checks are given the student covering care of equipment.
Final Phase Check Grade   5
Turrets, Turret Manipulation, and Sighting grades are included in Final Phase Check Grade.

I ACKNOWLEDGE THAT I HAVE RECEIVED THE TRAINING AS SHOWN ABOVE	I CERTIFY THAT THE ABOVE ENTRIES ARE CORRECT AND TRAINING HAS BEEN COMPLETED AS INDICATED
SIGNATURE OF INDIVIDUAL	SIGNATURE OF COMMANDING OFFICER
Donell Mathews	E.L. Harring 1st. Lt. A.C.

* Completed but not Graded.

These photographs show a gunnery training report card and a certificate a gunner would have been issued upon successful completion of gunnery training. The intensive training didn't bother soldiers like Stanley Vaughan, even thought he described it as "exhausting." Indeed, Vaughan still wasn't completely prepared for what he faced when he was deployed to the Pacific theater. "Buckingham was one of my first experiences in planes," he said bittersweetly. "But I didn't learn the fear of planes until I went overseas and saw them crashing all around me. We lost lots and lots of men."

ARMY AIR FORCES FLEXIBLE GUNNERY SCHOOL
FORT MYERS, FLORIDA

Certificate of Proficiency
Be it known that

Has satisfactorily completed a forty-eight (48) hour short course in_____ turrets, has passed a written examination, and is qualified to perform first echelon maintenance on these turrets.

RICHARD R. WAUGH
LT. COLONEL - AIR CORPS.
DIRECTOR OF TRAINING

Heavy bombers during World War II flew at tremendous heights, and many enemy targets were bombed from altitudes in the 30,000-foot range. Pilots, navigators, gunners, and other crewmembers on bombers all needed to use oxygen equipment to survive at these heights, and altitude training was an integral part of the BAAF experience. These men are seen sitting in a special altitude trainer, a sealed room where the exact conditions at 30,000 feet could be experienced. B-17 bombers were also used at BAAF and took gunnery students on actual flights into the sub-stratosphere. Below is a BAAF altitude training card dating from late in the war—June 1945. Issued to a private, it appears to indicate he successfully completed his altitude flight training.

ALTITUDE TRAINING ACTIVITY
BUCKINGHAM ARMY AIR FIELD
FORT MYERS, FLORIDA

DATE 6-2-45

NAME _Ries, George E._

A.S.N. _15407456_ RANK _Pvt._

FLIGHT TYPE 1 _Comp_ TYPE 2 _Comp_.

REMARKS

SIGNED _H J Hester Capt_

Form 1   AVIATION PHYSIOLOGIST

Students at the Flexible Gunnery School at BAAF were expected to know their weapons inside and out. If a gun jammed or malfunctioned at 30,000 feet, a gunner needed to be able to disassemble it, fix it, and put it back together so as to keep on firing. BAAF had a special training area known as the Malfunction Range, where guns with defects awaited gunners. It was up to the students to find the trouble with each gun within a specified amount of time. The men also needed to be able to do this delicate work in the dark, lest something happen on a night mission. Gunners practiced these potentially life-saving skills while blindfolded with handkerchiefs. Here men practice assembling a .50 caliber machine gun while blindfolded. Cleaning and taking proper care of guns were also stressed.

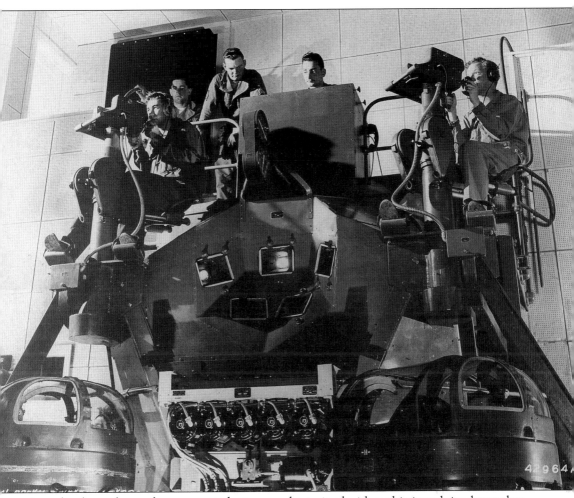

As technology advanced, gunnery students were also trained with sophisticated simulators that used film footage of planes and allowed students to track and score in realistic air battles. This was considered more realistic than shooting at slow moving, towed targets. Known as the Waller Gunnery Trainers, the devices were invented by Fred Waller and the Vitarama Corporation and helped improve students' rate of fire and accuracy. The Waller Gunnery Trainer used five 35-millimeter projectors mounted together that projected onto a hemispherical screen. It had four gunners' stations. Two of them simulated the bomber's top turret, and two were used for side, nose, or tail training. The gun stations recoiled when fired, just like a real turret gun, and the students wore headphones that played sounds of guns firing and aircraft noises. The goal was to make the simulation as realistic as possible. (Courtesy of David Strohmaier.)

The gunners fired their "virtual" gun at projections on a screen, and a photoelectric system scored their "hits." The image at left shows the complicated mechanics needed to make the device function. It was estimated that 1 hour of training on the Waller device was the equivalent of 10 hours of practice in the air. Calculations done after the war estimated that some 350,000 lives were saved due to the skills learned using the trainer. Photographs exist of the cement block foundation that once housed the enormous Waller Gunnery Trainers at Buckingham AAF. This foundation can still be found amidst the tall grasses and palmetto trees on the former base property. (Both, courtesy of David Strohmaier.)

Another critical element of gunnery training was learning to recognize enemy planes. Even more critical was learning their shapes and silhouettes, as that was often all a gunner could see in a bright, sunlit sky. On a motion picture screen, silhouettes of various enemy planes would flash for 1/25th of a second—planes such as the Bf-109, the Focke-Wolfe 190, and the Mitsubishi A6M, also known as the Zero. Students had to be able to instantly identify them. In the skies, there's no time to ponder whether a plane is an ally or an enemy. Model airplanes were also used to help gunners become familiar with the details of various aircraft—friend and foe. When weather conditions prevented outdoor training, time was spent indoors working on plane identification.

Since many practice flights took place out over the waters of the Gulf of Mexico, BAAF had rescue boats stationed on the coast. The army's crash boat bases were located at Marco Island and on the Caloosahatchee River in Fort Myers, according to army documents dating to just after the war. Some veterans recall a crash boat base on Fort Myers Beach, but there is no apparent documentation of this locale. If a plane from BAAF or other nearby bases ditched in the Gulf, crash boat crews stood ready to rescue downed airmen.

Crews practiced for water rescues that would inevitably come when a plane crash-landed in the water. "Our practice range was out over the Gulf," said Oscar Corbin Jr. "If a plane went down out there, a rescue mission had to go and get them." In this series of photographs, a soldier is strapped into a basket of sorts attached to a crane or winch. His life preserver still in place, he is ready to be hoisted up to the rescue boat and carefully pulled on board.

Besides being ready to rescue any downed crews, the men on the crash boats may have helped BAAF trainees prepare for the possibility of a crash into the sea. Soldiers were taught that a simple G.I. barracks bag could be filled with air and used as a life preserver. A pair of trousers tied off at the legs could serve the same purpose. Life rafts, no matter the size, could be used to rescue large numbers of downed aviators. Even small life rafts such as this could accommodate up to a dozen people until they could be rescued. Despite the open water nearby, much of this training took place in the base swimming pool or in a waterhole on the base known as the "ditching pond."

According to historical articles written by former Buckingham gunnery instructor Paul Fleming Jr., planes were dispatched on separate runways at the same time, one after another, starting at 8:00 a.m. and again at 1:00 p.m. The goal was to get at least 40 aircraft airborne within 30 minutes.

Paul Fleming Jr. said that there were usually two instructors per 10 to 12 students aboard a bomber. Hooked up to oxygen, the plane would ascend to 22,000 feet and fire at tow targets being pulled by planes. Women, who were part of the WASP program, piloted many of these planes. It took up to an hour to reach altitude and then another hour for each student to take his turn at the various gun positions.

A tow target wasn't the most effective method, according to Paul Fleming Jr. "The target merely sat there a couple of hundred feet away," Fleming wrote in a report about his army experience. "The benefit was in firing guns at a high altitudes with oxygen on. Also, the ammunition used for these exercises was training grade, not good enough for combat but more than adequate for training." (Courtesy of David Stallman.)

"A lot of jams were encountered and these were cleared while encumbered by the oxygen mask and the cold of altitude," wrote Paul Fleming Jr. After the high-altitude training, students were in for a different kind of treat. The plane would descend to a mere 500 feet or so over the blue Gulf waters. Students would fire into the water creating large splashes, and then they would target and shoot their own splash. The tow planes in these photographs are being piloted by women from the WASP program. (Courtesy of David Stallman.)

At the end of five or six weeks of training, reports say that the new incoming class of students would gather for a special ceremony with the outgoing graduates who were headed overseas. Green soldiers fresh from high school, family farms, and football teams met with men their own age seasoned by weeks of intense, often frightening training who were going off to war.

Paul Fleming Jr. said that at the end of a six-week training course at BAAF, students received a pair of wings. The award resembled a winged bullet. Humorously, Fleming says that some graduating gunners would go and buy extra sets of wings at the base's Post Exchange to pass out to their girlfriends.

Four

SOARING SKYWARD
FIGHTERS AND BOMBERS

The main goal of Buckingham's Flexible Gunnery School was to train students to be aerial gunners who would fly as part of a crew on army bombers. Their mission was to man the bomber's gun turrets and protect the aircraft from enemy planes. While much of gunnery training took place on the ground, planes of every shape and size were as common as Florida mosquitoes in the skies over Buckingham.

Various archival and modern materials related to Buckingham show an impressive list of planes that were either stationed at or visited BAAF. A common one was the AT-6 Texan (also known as the T-6), which appears in these photographs. Others included the similar BT-13 Valiant, the AT-18, the AT-23, the RB-34, the P-39 Airacobra, and the P-63 King Cobra.

The bombers and gunnery students at Buckingham sometimes reportedly worked hand-in-hand with the fighter pilots based over at Page Field, a nearby base known as Fort Myers AAF. The fighters would engage in mock attacks on the bombers from BAAF. Many of these practice battles took place over the Gulf of Mexico, where sections were set aside for military training. Fishermen in the area were warned to stay away.

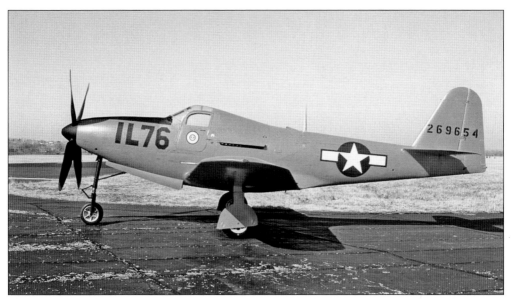

There are nerve-wracking tales of "flying pinballs" at BAAF. As the stories go, shooting at banners towed behind a plane sometimes wasn't enough. Instead, heavily armored planes would take to the sky with what must have been some of the bravest pilots ever. Gunnery students would actually shoot at these armored planes to get experience firing at real planes. The flying pinball was usually based on a regular P-63 airplane, seen in the first photograph. According to military aviation experts, there were some 330 specially modified P-63As and P63-Cs, which the U.S. Army Air Force used as manned targets. They carried about one ton of extra external armor plating. The practicing gunnery students fired a special "frangible" bullet made of graphite and lead. These bullets shattered on impact, thus doing less damage to the aircraft than a regular bullet. (Above, courtesy of National Museum of the U.S. Air Force.)

These photographs show the popular P-51 Mustang, one of the workhorses of the U.S. Army Air Forces. This long-range, single-seat fighter aircraft was armed with six .50 caliber M2 Browning machine guns. External fuel tanks allowed the P-51 to travel great distances and accompany bombers on flights over enemy territory. Planes such as the P-51 would have been a common sight at nearby Page Field, where the army trained fighter pilots. However, they also certainly were a part of the fleet at Buckingham AAF, where they might have been used in pilot training, mock battles, and even as tow planes for aerial targets.

Bombers of every shape and size crisscrossed Buckingham's runways and skyways. The B-17 Flying Fortress, seen here, was a four-engine heavy bomber used heavily in bombing runs over Germany. The B-17 quickly became a favorite of bomber crews, especially for its legendary reputation for withstanding serious damage. There are many tales of shot-up B-17s safely returning from missions over Germany. At the war's end, it was estimated that the B-17 dropped more bombs on Germany than any other army airplane. The model was also used in the Pacific to a lesser extent. Other bombers that were used in training at Buckingham included the B-18 Bolo, B-24 Liberator, B-25 Mitchell, B-26 Marauder, and B-29 Superfortress.

The B-24 Liberator bomber, seen here at BAAF, is the most-produced military aircraft in history. Considered more modern than the B-17, it was also more difficult to fly, and many crews preferred the B-17. Being an aerial gunner on a bomber brought additional risks beyond the basic threat of being shot down by enemy airplanes. Veterans from Buckingham Army Air Field tell stories of gunners who ended up trapped in their bubble-like turrets beneath their damaged planes. For example, perhaps the electrical systems would fail or the gunner was injured and unable to work the controls that allowed the gunner to re-enter the plane. Pilots would stall as long as possible, as crewmen tried to rescue the trapped gunner, but sometimes they had to land with the turret down, crushing it and the gunner inside. "I had it happen to me when I was in Europe," said BAAF pilot Tommy Doyle. "There was a little space between the ground and the turret. We had a gunner in there, and he just made it."

The B-25 Mitchell was a twin-engine medium bomber named after Gen. Billy Mitchell, a famed military aviator. Due to the small size of electric gun turrets on many bombers, there were size limitations for aerial gunnery students. Each man had to be 5 feet, 8 inches or smaller and 170 pounds or less. Students also had to be between 18 and 30 years old. Originally, gunners were all volunteers, but as the need for aerial gunners increased, this requirement was dropped.

Sometimes "guest" airplanes would put in an appearance at Buckingham Army Air Field, such as this odd-looking Catalina OA-10. The OA-10 was an American flying boat used primarily in anti-submarine warfare, convoy escorts, search-and-rescue missions, and cargo transport. This OA-10 was not stationed at BAAF; rather, it was moved there for three days to avoid a hurricane that was threatening its home base in Mississippi.

In his memoir *One Man's Destiny*, veteran Thomas C. Wilcox recalled his time training aboard an old B-18 Bolo bomber at BAAF and shooting at tow targets in the skies over Southwest Florida. He says instructors always stressed the importance of attaching the chute—a foot-long canvas bag—to the side of the gun in order to catch the ejected brass shell casings. To add emphasis, the instructor relayed a harrowing story. "This very nervous gunner took his turn at the machine gun and when he put in a new belt of ammo, he forgot to fasten the chute to catch the brass," Wilcox wrote. "The pilot noticed that and pulled back on the throttles to quiet the engines and yelled, 'Fasten your chute and save your brass!' The nervous gunner bailed out [of the plane]. After they fished him out of the Gulf, they asked him why he bailed out. He said, 'The plane's engines were stopping, and the pilot told me to fasten my chute and save my ass, so I did.' "

During and after the war, lots of information about the work done at Buckingham was restricted. This was definitely true of reports of crashes and fatalities during training. Too many incidents could hurt troop morale and embolden an enemy. However, a number of photographs showing plane accidents at Buckingham and nearby Page Field exist, including the ones seen on these pages. "That's one of my horrible memories," said Georgilee Elmore, a nurse at the base hospital. "We had a B-17 crash, and they brought in all the young kids that were burned. I took ahold of one man's arm, and his skin just came off in my hand."

Other veterans recall the time an inexperienced pilot flew his AT-6 into the side of the building at BAAF, and then moments later, a bomber flew just over the base hospital and exploded. The crews of both planes were killed. Another time, a B-24 crashed on approach, killing everyone on board except one soldier who was thrown clear and was basically unhurt.

Retired aerial gunner Fred Schlosstein once told the *Lehigh Acres Citizen* that many young men were killed at BAAF during training. "But none of that was told then because of censorship. No one knew about the deaths of the boys who came to be trained . . . nothing was ever given out about the [base]," he said.

Five

THE DAILY DRILL
LIFE ON THE BASE

Life at Buckingham Army Air Field was certainly a mixed bag. Some veterans have fond memories of good times with army buddies, dances, beaches, and even celebrity USO visits. Others say they were too busy for fun and mainly remember serious training, inhospitable conditions, and the looming shadow of war. Daily life at Buckingham was just such a combination—occasional frivolity amidst life-and-death drama.

Buckingham AAF had its own newspaper, called the *Flexigun*. An issue dated May 1, 1943, gives a wonderful sampling of the many ways BAAF was like a small town. The paper is filled with ads for businesses in Fort Myers, such as the Franklin Arms Hotel, Parker's Book Store, and Goff's Jewelry. There are ads for the three movie theaters in the town, which were the Arcade, the Ritz, and the Edison. Movies playing included *Andy Hardy's Double Life*, *Bambi*, *Immortal Sergeant*, and No. 13 in the Captain Midnight series. Front-page stories covered both the latest achievements and changes in gunnery training, as well as a story about Mother's Day gifts being available at the Post Exchange. Local girl scouts were helping with the wrapping of presents. Inside there were humorous news tidbits from around the base, notes from the base administrators, and a sports story about two of the BAAF baseball teams that were meeting for a championship game. The base band was going to perform at the match. (Courtesy of Lee County Mosquito Control.)

This photograph shows a small convenience store at Buckingham AAF. On military bases, the PX or Post Exchange is a store for military personnel and their families. They are sometimes also called BXs, or Base Exchanges. While modern PXs are akin to a big department store, in decades past, they were often more like a trading post. They would have cold drinks, cigarettes, stamps, magazines, assorted toiletries, and the like. In this photograph, Colgate toothpaste is on the shelves. Other items visible include Dreft and Rinso laundry soaps, Chesterfield cigarettes, Burma Shave shaving cream, Aspergum analgesic chewing gum, products named Argo and Red Top, and a sign advertising "Fresh milk for 10¢ a pint." Of course, peeking from behind the counter is a cooler filled with the ubiquitous glass bottles of Coca-Cola.

A different stand at the base sells a variety of magazines and newspapers. Many of the periodicals appear to be pulp-fiction-type stories of adventure and romance. Titles on the counter include *Real Stories, True, Popular Sports, Detective Story Annual, Mammoth Detective, Action Stories, Thrilling Ranch Stories,* and a 10¢ *Sunday News* comics section with Dick Tracy on the front. The clerk in the photograph is identified as Florence Sciple.

Many women from the Fort Myers area found work at Buckingham AAF. While it may look like a typical 1940s office, there is one feature that stands out. On the wall at the top right of the photograph stands a "crash phone." The sign says "incoming calls only," and a wire runs from the phone to an alarm on the wall. When a Buckingham plane crashed, these women were ready to alert emergency personnel and commanding officers.

Hundreds of civilian employees would make their way to the base each day for work. Many of them were mechanics and maintenance crews, who were a critical component of the success of Buckingham Army Air Field. It was their job to keep the planes flying and the guns firing. Crews often worked overnight shifts in order to make sure planes were ready for training runs in the morning. The mechanics' work depot included a complete welding shop, a riveting shop, and a machine shop.

These photographs appear to show military couples at Buckingham Army Air Field. Veterans who trained at BAAF have been quoted saying that they were too busy to date while at the base. However, certainly romances must have been struck between permanent personnel. There are numerous tales of service men meeting their future wives while at BAAF, but most of those stories involve soldiers meeting civilians from the area. Today most regulations regarding fraternization focus on the importance of officers and the enlisted ranks not becoming too social. Of course, there are also strict rules against fraternizing with the enemy.

"Soldiers Are Religious" is the headline on a page in a Buckingham AAF yearbook, which was put out for base personnel. The page features images of the base's churches. The photograph above shows what appears to be a Catholic service underway. The kneeling men in the photograph are all wearing dress military uniforms. Aerial photographs of the base show at least two churches standing right at the main circle, which was located in the center of the base. Men and women of many faiths served at Buckingham, and just like in any city, there were several different places to worship. The base's newspaper listed services for Catholics, Protestants, Christian Scientists, Jews, and, tellingly, a "Colored Service."

Thousands of Jews served in the U.S. military during World War II, and Buckingham was home to many of them. Thus Jewish services were also a part of the daily life on the base. This photograph of a 1944 service at BAAF comes from the Florida State Archives and was originally in the collection of the Jewish Museum of Florida in Miami. (Courtesy of Florida State Archives.)

Just as today, soldiers during World War II could often be found relaxing with a game of pool. This was likely taken at a recreational hall or club for enlisted men. On bases such as BAAF, it was common for personnel of different ranks to have their own social areas—again to help avoid improper fraternization. Officers had their clubs. NCOs, or non-commissioned officers, had theirs.

There were reportedly seven mess halls around the large base. While few people today know for sure what the food was like, there is little doubt that food was being prepared on a massive scale each day for tens of thousands of hungry officers, soldiers, WACs, and civilians. Veteran Stanley Vaughan recalls being constantly congested due to the damp air and frequent altitude changes while flying. "Each morning when we awoke, the night air had brought moisture enough through the openings for windows to make your bed completely wet," Vaughan wrote in a memoir. "Adding the flying, ascending, and descending to that meant my ears were stopped up the entire time I was there. I never tasted a bite of food . . . and for the first time in my life, eating became boring."

In this first photograph, WACs in a recruiting parade march past the Bradford Hotel, the Arcade Theatre, and Sears Roebuck and Company in downtown Fort Myers on November 13, 1943. There are a good number of images of parades and assemblies in the nearby town featuring military personnel from Buckingham Army Air Field. Fort Myers got behind the war effort and supported the men and women of the base. Homes were opened to soldiers and families needing lodging. Much of the town's population either worked at the base or provided services there. Parades such as these may have been for recruiting purposes, to mark holidays such as Veteran's Day, and certainly to thank the townsfolk who were so kind to these new arrivals. (Above, courtesy of the Reva Ingram Fortune Papers, Betty H. Carter Women Veterans Historical Project, University of North Carolina, Greensboro.)

This photograph was labeled "M.P.s marching down street." Like something out of a Norman Rockwell painting, the proud military men in their best dress uniform, complete with gloves, march in unison down a Fort Myers street. The base band follows them. The sun is shining, palm trees are swaying, and two boys merrily ride along on their bikes, following the army unit through town.

Life at Buckingham was hardly dignified. The niceties from home went out the window in Southwest Florida. "After several days of sun and rain, many of us broke out with what was at first diagnosed as chicken pox," Thomas C. Wilcox recalled in his memoirs. "As it turned out, we were afflicted with prickly heat rash caused by the heat and high humidity. Many of us also got 'jock itch,' which the Doc treated with silver nitrate."

The following photographs from BAAF show light-hearted events during typical days at the base: a soldier joking around with fake, bulging eyes and women looking at puppies that were born under a building. While serious training was the order of the day, there were also quirky moments at Buckingham. In his memoirs, Thomas C. Wilcox recalls a minnow mystery that surrounded each rainfall. "At first, we thought it rained fish, because during and after a rain, they appeared in every puddle of water and swam in little streams that came from the runoff from the barrack's roof. What we learned was, the little fish came up out of the sand when it rained and burrowed back down when it quit. . . . There they hibernated until the next rain."

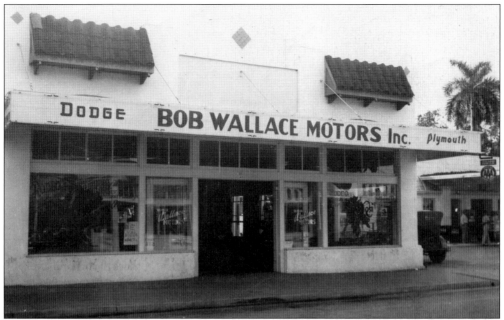

The bus from Buckingham would drop off servicemen at this Dodge Motors store in Fort Myers for a day of fun in the "big city." Of course, Buckingham AAF was actually a bigger "city" than Fort Myers was at the time. "Fort Myers was a small town," veteran Fred Schlosstein said in an interview with the *Lehigh Acres Citizen*. "But the boys did like to go over there and have fun. . . . They called us the boys from Buckingham."

Soldiers and WACs would go into town on weekends when big dances, and socials would be held at different places downtown. Popular venues included the Elks Club and the pavilion that would later become the Hall of 50 States, as well as a nightclub called Rendezvous, located near the historic Post Office Building in Fort Myers. Others would cross the Edison Bridge to North Fort Myers, where establishments such as the North Shore Club and the Town Hall Club awaited.

Many of the servicemen at Buckingham enjoyed getting away to area beaches when time permitted. Carloads could often be seen heading down to Fort Myers Beach or Bonita Beach, sometimes with G.I.s standing on the running boards or hanging on to the side of the car. These fun seekers were usually permanent base personnel, since veterans who attended gunnery school at BAAF say that they seldom had the time or energy for much recreation after long days of intense training.

Black servicemen had their own places to relax in Fort Myers, many of them located in the historically black neighborhoods along Anderson Avenue, today Martin Luther King Jr. Boulevard. No club on this street was more famous than McCollum Hall, which housed a large stage and dance hall on the second floor. During World War II, the United Services Organization, or USO, used McCollum Hall to entertain black troops from Buckingham and Page Field.

Duke Ellington, seen here in 1943 at the Hurricane Club in New York City, along with Louis Armstrong, B. B. King, and other famous performers appeared at McCollum Hall over the years. Popular big band groups also regularly performed here, and during the days of Buckingham, it was not uncommon to see white civilians and soldiers turn out to the hall as well, drawn by these famous musicians. In fact, McCollum Hall was one of the few places in Florida that was at least somewhat integrated. However, areas of the hall were still separated by ropes in order to keep a division of races, especially on the dance floor. As the evening wore on, the ropes would fall to the wayside, and everyone would be dancing together. This was nearly unheard of in the South and in Fort Myers, where segregation was still the norm. (Courtesy of the Library of Congress.)

Originally built in 1938, McCollum Hall still stands in downtown Fort Myers, although it has long since fallen into disrepair. The second floor, where so many greats played, became a rooming house in the 1980s. Historic preservationists and city leaders have long worked on plans to revitalize this landmark building.

PL 4G106-2   COUPLES   DANCING BAAF FT. MYERS FLA.

Back at Buckingham Field, the Special Service Department was an army unit that had the assignment of looking after the "welfare, recreation, and physical fitness" of the base's personnel. In other words, they were the people in charge of making sure officers and soldiers relaxed during what was otherwise often a very intense and trying job. Regular socials and dances were planned and held for the men and women of the base. They also offered educational opportunities, such as foreign language classes. Morale boosting programs were distributed via post radio, camp newspapers, special films, posters, public speakers, and even cartoons.

Certainly one of the most popular aspects of life in the military and at Buckingham was the regular entertainment provided by the USO. Hundreds of big-name movie stars, musicians, and sports stars donated their time and talents during World War II to entertain the troops. In these historic Buckingham photographs are Hollywood's beloved actress Judy Garland, funny man and actor Danny Kaye, and baseball great Leo Durocher. The USO disbanded after World War II, but it returned to active duty with start of the Korean War. It's stayed in service ever since, providing entertainment and boosting morale for generations of servicemen and -women.

McCoy Park was the base's ball field. In this photograph, the stands are full. The soldiers always looked forward to the games between the BAAF teams and visitors from other military bases each week. "They had a couple of baseball teams," said veteran BAAF pilot Tommy Doyle. "One fellow was a pitcher. He left the service and was picked up by a major league team. I can't recall his name, but I watched him pitch, and he was really a fireball."

The rhythms of daily life continued at BAAF for three years—from reveille and raising the flag in the morning until "lights out" at night. Despite the rigors of army life, there were sweet moments to be had that stayed with some veterans long after the war. "Buckingham was near many orange groves," recalled Georgilee Elmore. "When the orange blossoms started blooming, it was one of the most wonderful smells, all those orange blossoms. Every time I smell an orange blossom, I think of Buckingham Field."

Six

AFTER THE WAR
BUCKINGHAM TODAY

All along, it was known that Buckingham would have a limited lifespan. The army had designated it as a temporary base from the start. In the months after the war, in late summer 1945, all base personnel assumed that Buckingham would close. Indeed, operations slowed down dramatically, and training was suspended.

ARMY AIR FORCES

Certificate of Appreciation

FOR WAR SERVICE

TO

Mariam T. Lenig

I CANNOT *meet you personally to thank you for a job well done; nor can I hope to put in written words the great hope I have for your success in future life.*

Together we built the striking force that swept the Luftwaffe from the skies and broke the German power to resist. The total might of that striking force was then unleashed upon the Japanese. Although you no longer play an active military part, the contribution you made to the Air Forces was essential in making us the greatest team in the world.

The ties that bound us under stress of combat must not be broken in peacetime. Together we share the responsibility for guarding our country in the air. We who stay will never forget the part you have played while in uniform. We know you will continue to play a comparable role as a civilian. As our ways part, let me wish you God speed and the best of luck on your road in life. Our gratitude and respect go with you.

COMMANDING GENERAL
ARMY AIR FORCES

When the orders came to deactivate the base, personnel started transferring elsewhere, and civilians went and found new jobs. Plans for the base's closing called for three officers and approximately 180 civilians to stay and manage the property until the army turned the station and land back over to Lee County.

An army report estimated that approximately $126 million was spent operating BAAF during its 39 months of active duty. The estimated value of the base and planes when BAAF closed was $65 million. As the army ended its time in Southwest Florida, there were lots of rumors of new, unused equipment being shoved into trenches and buried. These rumors persisted for years, but most say they are urban legends.

For a short time after the war, barracks at BAAF were used as classrooms for the school that today is Edison State College. The school moved out in 1948. Many of the base's runways were torn up, and the Ocala limestone under them was used to help lay out other area roadways. Other portions likely ended up covered in brush and are still there today. Tommy Doyle was a pilot who returned from overseas duty and was assigned to Buckingham. When the war ended, the U.S. Army was left with far more military equipment than it needed in peacetime. To this end, one of Doyle's assignments was to fly many of the base's B-24s to an "airplane graveyard" near Altus, Oklahoma.

After Tommy Doyle was discharged from the army in 1949, he returned to the Fort Myers area. The old Buckingham AAF property was being dismantled, and Doyle got into business with Charlie Flint. Their new endeavor was moving buildings. They bid on contracts with the army and ended up transporting many of the base's buildings elsewhere. "An old army truck was used to pull them, and we had a 30-foot or 40-foot trailer and very crude equipment that got them jacked up, so we could move them all over the place," Doyle recalled. "We moved one of the barrack buildings to LaBelle. It was the city hall up there for years. There were several moved right into Fort Myers and used as homes. They rebuilt a lot of them." This was the start of Flint and Doyle Structural Movers, a company that continues to serve the Southwest Florida community to this day.

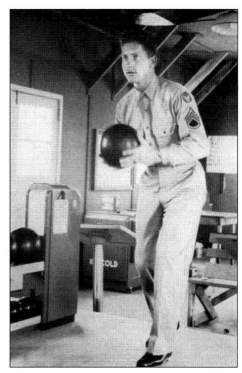

One of the greatest legacies of Buckingham AAF to Fort Myers and the surrounding communities was the large number of military men and women who later settled in this area. Some came soon after the war, and others came decades later when they retired. Their impact has been felt in big and small ways. A few examples include the aforementioned Tommy Doyle, as well as former Fort Myers mayor Oscar Corbin Jr.; former school board member John Beckett; local real estate agent Marvin Mulkey; and the former president of the Lee County Bank, Malcolm Schroeder. The list goes on and on.

In various forms, traces of Buckingham lived on. The Dome Restaurant was one of the most famous landmarks in Bonita Springs, which was southwest of the base. Built in the early 1940s, the bottom portion of the Dome was constructed using ammunition boxes left over from the Buckingham gunnery school. Covered with coral rock, the structure was capped with a bright orange roof and topped by a green leaf. It was torn down in 1992 to make room for road improvements. (Courtesy of Bonita Springs Historical Society.)

In 1968, the fast-growing Lee County Mosquito Control District moved its headquarters from Fort Myers to the former BAAF property. By this time, the base's runways were long gone, as were most of the base's buildings. What was once a 7,000-acre site was now just 250 acres.

The Lee County Mosquito Control District was created in January 1958. It consolidated three existing mosquito control areas and brought most of the county under one umbrella organization. With Lee County's swampy landscape, mosquitoes were long the bane of residents and visitors alike. But new mosquito control techniques made life here more livable and was one key factor in Florida's rapid population growth in the 1950s and 1960s.

This aerial photograph, taken from directly above the Mosquito Control complex, shows a line of DC-3s on the runway, which was once the main apron at Buckingham Army Air Field. Looking at the center of the photograph, the rectangular building seen below and to the left of the large gravel loop road is an original BAAF warehouse, the only base building that remains intact from the war years. (Both, courtesy of Lee County Mosquito Control.)

Today the Lee County Mosquito Control District has more than 80 permanent employees and 30 part-time employees. They study and track mosquito populations across Lee County and fly a fleet of airplanes and helicopters that aim to reduce the mosquito populations, particularly in populated areas. Many of the helicopters the agency uses are army surplus, some dating to the Vietnam War. They are outfitted with large sprayers, and the "helos" can often be seen swooping and diving over wooded and marshy areas of Lee County spraying larvicides. The planes in the photographs are part of Mosquito Control's fleet of DC-3s. (Both, courtesy of Lee County Mosquito Control.)

Today there is just one original base building left on the property. It is this old warehouse made of hard pine located near the main entrance gate to the Mosquito Control compound. Walking through it, it is easy to picture the soldiers and civilians who worked here during the war. The photograph below shows the inside of the Mosquito Control District warehouse. For many years, the building was used to store old pesticide drums. Those are gone now, and more recently, it has been used to house aircraft engines and other assorted aircraft parts.

BUCKINGHAM ARMY AIR FIELD

built by U.S. Corps of Engineers in 1942

Buckingham Army Air Field
1942-1945

2117TH BASE UNIT

Early in 1942, the United States Government leased 6,500 acres of mostly brush, palmetto trees, and in some places, pine stumps left from previous logging operations, to establish a flexible gunnery training school on this site. Construction of the training center began in February 1942. By June, 1,200 men were working 10 hours a day to have the field ready for operations. The field was formally activated on July 5, 1942. Classes began on September 7, 1942, even though field construction was far from complete. At the peak of its operation, the field was home to 16,000 people and consisted of almost 700 buildings.

Initially, bomber gunners went through a five-week training program. They were trained to maintain, disassemble and effectively fire .30 and .50 caliber machine guns. These guns were used to defend bomber aircraft such as the B-17, B-24 and B-29 from enemy fighter planes. Both trap and skeet shooting ranges were used to develop aiming skills. Students were also trained on the moving target range riding in Jeeps, simulator training, and in the final week, air to air gunnery shooting at targets towed by aircraft.

Various aircraft were used to perform the training mission at the field. They included the AT-6, AT-18, AT-23, RB-34, P-39, B-17, B-24 and B-29.

The field was closed on September 30, 1945. Fifty thousand gunners had graduated from the program. In addition, the field had trained co-pilots for the B-17, B-24 and B-29 bombers. The field made a significant contribution to victory in World War II.

A commemorative sign reads in part: "Early in 1942, the United States Government leased 6,5000 acres of mostly brush, palmetto trees, and in some places, pine stumps left from previous logging operations, to establish a flexible gunnery training school on this site. . . . At the peak of its operation, the field was home to 16,000 people and consisted of almost 700 buildings. . . . The field was closed on September 30, 1945. Fifty thousand gunners had graduated from the program. In addition, the field had trained co-pilots for the B-17, B-24, and B-29 bombers. The field made a significant contribution to victory in World War II."

Out on the apron—the cement pad that surrounds an airport where planes taxi and park—there are still chunks of foundation and long metal strips cutting through the cement field. These are the remnants of what was once a BAAF hangar or repair shop. The metal strips were likely runners for the large hangar doors. For the staff at Lee County Mosquito Control District, these artifacts are a constant reminder of the long-gone base. "You have this fondness for this place—that it was such a pivotal place and time in so many people's lives. It gives you a sense of pride," said Shelly Redovan, the district's deputy director of education and communication. "Who wants to work in a modern office building that has no past compared to a place that has a tremendous amount of devotion and dedication and service around it."

This wide shot of the BAAF apron was once filled with planes of all shapes and sizes during World War II. While this was a place for planes to park during the war, today the old BAAF apron is used as the main runway for Mosquito Control planes. Here at the edge of the Mosquito Control property, it's easy to see how many of the surrounding Lehigh Acres neighborhoods are actually built on top of what was once BAAF property. The cement from the BAAF apron extends right past the Mosquito Control fence and into a homeowner's backyard. Many of the surrounding houses and streets are platted right on top of the old BAAF runways.

If a visitor looks closely at the huge cement apron at the Mosquito Control property, he or she will quickly note the many small hourglass-shaped notches in the cement. Many still have a small metal bar embedded in them. These are tie-downs that are left over from the days of the Buckingham Army Air Field. Just as it is done at small airports today, ropes and cables, which were fixed to the ground, were attached to warplanes in order to keep them securely in place when not in use and, especially, in times of high winds or inclement weather. There were far more planes than there were hangars or garages at the base, so tie-downs would have been very important. In fact, most planes at Buckingham AAF were always parked outside, except when they needed to go in for maintenance or repairs.

These photographs show a thick-walled room that is located inside another Mosquito Control warehouse. The warehouse was built on top of an old BAAF foundation that most likely was an armament building. At the center of this foundation, this room stood with dense cement walls more than a foot thick. This was likely a room for holding ordnance of some sort, and the thick walls were meant to protect people lest there be an explosion. Mosquito Control officials wanted to remove the bunker when they built their new warehouse, but after several failed attempts, it was left intact, and the warehouse was built around it.

This photograph shows the current fish house at the Mosquito Control headquarters. It's used to hold fish that are part of hyacinth control, which also operates from the Mosquito Control property. Indeed Lee County has its own agency devoted to controlling this fast-growing, non-native species, which crowds out native water plants. In this photograph, one can see a low cement berm running along the edge of the room. That is yet another portion of a foundation left over from the Buckingham Army Air Field days. This building was constructed on top of an existing World War II–era foundation. Many other empty cement slabs and foundations sit on Mosquito Control property.

This view shows Homestead Road in the modern-day community of Lehigh Acres, once a main road running through the heart of Buckingham Army Air Field. It led all the way to the main airport area, just as today it leads to the Mosquito Control District headquarters. This private home that is located on Homestead Road, just west of the current Mosquito Control property, used to be in the center of the BAAF. In fact, Mosquito Control employees say this was where the original base bank was located. The bank was a small building, approximately 20 feet by 30 feet. After the war, it was used as a home. More recent owners expanded and built this larger house around the old bank building, which amazingly still stands inside.

Driving or walking along Homestead Road, a passerby might notice two odd stone bridges that run across a small ditch, but apparently lead to nowhere. These bridges are actually left over from the days of BAAF. According to Lee County Mosquito Control officials, they once led to the NCO Club, or Non-Commissioned Officers Club, which sat on the site. The stone appears to be lichen-covered coral, and the bridges are now covered with a carpet of grass. There are even pots at the end of the bridges, which likely once held flowers.

Even decades after the end of the war, there can still be mysteries surrounding Buckingham AAF. It has long been known that there were German prisoners of war held at various camps around Florida, including 225 POWs at Page Field, near U.S. 41 in Fort Myers. Some people who worked at Buckingham remember there were POWs interned there too. "They had an area for them [POWs], but they were pretty much free to move about and they did a lot of jobs out there," said former BAAF firefighter Harold Horne in a 1991 newspaper article. "I think most of them were glad to have been captured. They were treated well, and they ate good. You could tell them by the big 'PW' on the back of their work uniforms." (Courtesy of National Archives.)

Besides the many structural relics of Buckingham AAF still to be found around the area, there are also smaller, more personal items found that harken back to the war years. In the spring of 2010, a Mosquito Control employee named Donald Claytor Jr. was out sweeping an area of the former base when he came across a weathered 1941 German *reichspfennig*, a zinc coin from the Nazi era that had a prominent swastika on one side. Perhaps it belonged to a serviceman who had spent time in the European theater, or perhaps a German POW dropped it while digging ditches or doing other manual labor around Buckingham Army Air Field decades ago. (Both, courtesy of Donald Claytor Jr.)

This wasn't the first time Donald Claytor Jr. had found mementos of the past at the old Buckingham base property. Claytor got into metal detecting back in the 1970s, but his hobby really took off when he went to work for Mosquito Control. "I have been metal detecting these grounds for nearly 13 years and have made many interesting finds," Claytor said. "I first started searching around an old building foundation and, within minutes, I found a 1917 Mercury dime. Within the first week, I had found more old coins and relics than in all the previous years I had been metal detecting." These items include bracelets, rings, coins, pocket watches, shell casings, and other military adornments. (Courtesy of Donald Claytor Jr.)

One such find was a G.I.'s dog tag with a Catholic pendant attached to it. Claytor was able to track the name on the dog tag and found that it belonged to a Pvt. Charles J. Sweeney, who was a gunner aboard the "Temptation," a B-24 Liberator that was shot down during the first daylight bombing raid on the Philippines. While trying to return to base, it went down in the Davao Gulf. The entire crew perished. "It really amazes me how much stuff was lost in the short amount of time that the base was active," Claytor said. "There is a unique feeling [associated with finding] something that has been lost by someone who possibly gave up his life in defense of our country and knowing he was the last one to hold it in his hands." (Courtesy of Donald Claytor Jr.)

In July 2002, Lee County celebrated the 60th anniversary of the Buckingham Army Air Field. Participating organizations included the Southwest Florida Museum of History, the Florida Warbirds, the Lee County Board of Commissioners, Leadership Lee County, and the Lee County Mosquito Control District. This historical marker was put up at the intersection of Gunnery Boulevard and Sunset Road. The fence behind it marks the edge of Mosquito Control property, but once upon a time, this would have been smack dab in the heart of Buckingham AAF.

Just outside the main gates of the old BAAF and the current headquarters of Lee County Mosquito Control sits a most unusual neighborhood. It's called the Buckingham Air Park. Here it is just as likely to see an airplane driving down the street as a car. This is a "fly in" neighborhood, which means many homeowners have hangar-style garages attached to their homes to keep their personal planes. They taxi right out their driveway and over to the neighborhood runway, where they take off into the wild blue yonder.

The land where this neighborhood sits was once the heart of BAAF, and many of the streets in this quiet community sit right on top of streets that once were integral thoroughfares on the base. If a current aerial of the Buckingham Air Park were compared with an old map of the base (see page 15), many of the roadways would be nearly the same. At the entrance to the Buckingham Air Park, car drivers are warned that they must yield to planes and must not park within 30 feet of the street's centerline, since a wing might clip the roof of a car. (Above, courtesy of Lee County Property Appraiser.)

Exploring online satellite images of the area can turn up lots of secrets hidden from ground level. In this picture from the Lee County Property Appraiser's office, it's easy to see the faint remnants of many more BAAF roads and structures that are now abandoned and being overgrown by grass, trees, and brush. This fascinating photograph clearly shows the long, oval Ground Moving

Target Range tracks, just to the west of Buckingham Road. This was where countless Jeeps ran back and forth with white pieces of fabric fluttering in the breeze, acting as targets for countless aerial gunnery students who were learning how to shoot from moving vehicles. (Courtesy of Lee County Property Appraiser.)

Along Buckingham Road, there are obvious clues that there was once something much bigger here, but they are often overlooked. Some of these signs include cement blocks, metal latticework and bars, and crumbling foundations that are partially or completely hidden in the underbrush. These were once buildings, streets, and training centers at BAAF.

There is a local memorial to the men and women who trained and served in Lee County during World War II. It is located near the waters of the Caloosahatchee River in Centennial Park in downtown Fort Myers. It features three stone markers placed in front of a large airplane propeller. It honors all who served at Buckingham AAF and Page AAF.

In a 1943 yearbook for the personnel of BAAF, there is a passage that sums up perfectly what the base was all about: "And when this war is all over, Buckingham in all probability will be abandoned; its construction and buildings are temporary. But the men who have trained here will never forget the valuable things they have learned, and in the months ahead, the Nazis and the Japs will come to know better and better the accuracy of guns aimed by Buckingham men."

BUCKINGHAM AIR FIELD

BUCKINGHAM FIELD, A FLEXIBLE GUNNERY SCHOOL WAS ACTIVATED ON JULY 5, 1942. THE 65,723-ACRE BASE WAS LOCATED 6.5 MILES EAST OF FORT MYERS. BUCKINGHAM GRADUATED APPROXIMATELY 50,000 GUNNERS TO SERVE AMERICA'S W.W. II BOMBERS. AN INSTRUCTOR'S SCHOOL AND THE 75TH FLYING TRAINING WING WERE ALSO LOCATED THERE. DURING 1944-1945 B-29 PILOTS TRAINED AT THE BASE.

In the same 1943 Buckingham AAF yearbook, there is also the emotional poem "The Gunner's Vow," written by an anonymous author for aerial gunnery students at Buckingham and across the U.S. Army: "I wished to be a pilot, / And you along with me. / But if we all were pilots / Where would the Air Force be? / It takes GUTS to be a Gunner, / To sit out in the tail / When the Messerschmitts are coming / And the slugs begin to wail. / The pilot's just a chauffeur, / It's his job to fly the plane, / But it's WE who do the fighting, / Though we may not get the fame. / If we all must be Gunners / Then let us make this bet: / We'll be the best damn Gunners / That have left this station yet."

ABOUT THE ORGANIZATION

The Southwest Florida Museum of History opened in 1982 in the landmark Atlantic Coastline Railroad passenger depot, located in downtown Fort Myers. The museum is dedicated to the collection, preservation, and interpretation of history and traditions, with particular emphasis on Fort Myers and Southwest Florida. Featured exhibits include early Native American tribes, Spanish explorers, pioneering settlers of the Sunshine State's Gulf Coast, and the area's World War II history. The museum houses thousands of important artifacts from the region's past in its vast archives.

www.arcadiapublishing.com

MAP SEARCH

Discover books about the town where you grew up, the cities where your friends and families live, the town where your parents met, or even that retirement spot you've been dreaming about. Our Web site provides history lovers with exclusive deals, advanced notification about new titles, e-mail alerts of author events, and much more.

MADE IN THE USA

Arcadia Publishing, the leading local history publisher in the United States, is committed to making history accessible and meaningful through publishing books that celebrate and preserve the heritage of America's people and places. Consistent with our mission to preserve history on a local level, this book was printed in South Carolina on American-made paper and manufactured entirely in the United States.

This book carries the accredited Forest Stewardship Council (FSC) label and is printed on 100 percent FSC-certified paper. Products carrying the FSC label are independently certified to assure consumers that they come from forests that are managed to meet the social, economic, and ecological needs of present and future generations.

FSC
Mixed Sources
Product group from well-managed
forests and other controlled sources

Cert no. SW-COC-001530
www.fsc.org
© 1996 Forest Stewardship Council

Find Your Place in History.